✠ ✠ ✠

Maintaining Order In The Church

the roles of ushers, protocol officers and armor bearers

by

LANRE SOBO

Bloomington, IN Milton Keynes, UK

AuthorHouse™
1663 Liberty Drive, Suite 200
Bloomington, IN 47403
www.authorhouse.com
Phone: 1-800-839-8640

AuthorHouse™ UK Ltd.
500 Avebury Boulevard
Central Milton Keynes, MK9 2BE
www.authorhouse.co.uk
Phone: 08001974150

First published by AuthorHouse 7/18/2006

ISBN: 1-4259-4176-1 (sc)

Printed in the United States of America
Bloomington, Indiana

This book is printed on acid-free paper.

Lanre Sobo
927 Gillon Drive
Arlington, TX 76001
(1)-817 793 4140
(1)-817 468 1406
Ola_sobo@yahoo.co.uk

DEDICATION

This book is dedicated to my dearest wife Kemisola Sobo. Your love, encouragement, support, and prayers over the years have impacted my progress in life. My journey thus far in the Christian race is an indication of your determination that I succeed and excel in the assignments that the Lord has put in my hands.

I also wish to appreciate you for all the words of encouragement during the writing of this book. Your challenging repeated question to me on a daily basis *"When is the book going to be completed?"* provoked me to persevere to this point. Only God can honor and reward you in the measure that you truly deserve. You are truly a precious gift to me from God Almighty and I love you dearly.

I also dedicate this book to my children Lounrere and Lountodun whose presence around me give me joy, peace and happiness that constantly motivated me to complete the writing of this book. I really love you both. Thank you and God bless you.

Lanre

CONTENTS

ACKNOWLEDGEMENTS

I want to thank the Almighty God for saving my soul after several years of wandering in the wilderness of darkness, and for extending His amazing grace for me to write this book is in itself a miracle. Despite the challenges of my career, God still made it possible for this book to be written. I am very grateful to the Lord for this great testimony.

I also want to appreciate my Father in Lord Pastor Leke Sanusi who God used to open a chapter in my life from the first day I met him. I thank God for your life, your wife Pastor Bola Sanusi, your family, and my entire RCCG Victory House family. Those years of intensive and extensive trainings prepared me for this journey into destiny and for this I want to thank you.

In the pursuit of my destiny God re-directed my steps to the US, bringing me in contact with people I will regard as "Helpers of Destiny". First on that list is Pastor Ope Banwo, who is the catalyst used by God to inspire me to write a book. Whilst sharing ideas and vision with you as I served under your ministry in Omaha, NE, you urged me to write a book. Seeing you then as a young Pastor already writing your third book was a great source of encouragement to me. I am very grateful to you Sir. God bless you.

My appreciation goes to Pastors Ropo and Laide Tusin for the opportunity to serve under your ministry at RCCG Household of Faith Arlington, Texas in both ministerial and administrative capacities. I also appreciate the moral, and financial supports extended to my family just after relocating to Arlington, and while attending Bible College. May God bless both of you richly. I also acknowledge my entire RCCG Household of Faith Arlington family - you have all contributed to my life in a very positive way. God Bless you all.

I want to specifically thank Pastor Taiwo Ayeni of Rehoboth Bible Ministries, Arlington, Texas for the time and efforts spent towards the editing and publishing of this book. Despite my tiredness, your encouragement, prayers and writing skills motivated me to continue writing. Thank you very much Sir and I appreciate the gift of God in your life. God bless you.

I want to thank Pastor Adefope Folahan of Christ Assembly For All Nation (RCCG) for the time spent in proof reading the manuscript despite your busy schedule as a Parish Pastor. God reward your Labor in Jesus Name.

I am greatly indebted to some men of God who have over the years impacted my life by their life-styles, dedication to the word of God and the work of the ministry. These are in the persons of Pastor Enoch Adejare Adeboye - General Overseer of the Redeemed Christian Church of God (RCCG), Pastor Brown Oyitso –Provincial Pastor RCCG Lagos Nigeria, Rev. (Dr) Moses Aransiola – President, Gethsemane Prayer Ministries, Rev. and Pastor (Mrs.) Jonathan Adeboye - TOMG-NET Ministries, Ilorin, Nigeria, Rev. George Adegboye – General Overseer of Rhema Chapel Ministries, Pastor Biodun Coker - Zonal Coordinator, RCCG-NA, and Pastor Ajibike Akinkoye - President, Dove Media Group, Pastor Cal Lawa-

nson, Pastor O J Kuye of House on the Rock and
Pastor Chris Adetoro of Bread of Life Parish.

I really appreciate you all, may God reward you
in Jesus Name. Amen

FOREWORD

God is clearly not an author of confusion; rather, He is a God of order in His Church. I cannot imagine what the House of God would be without the anointed "enforcers" of order. Even our Lord Jesus Christ had to enforce order in the Temple when he chascd out those who had turned His Father's house into a 'den of thieves' - John 2:14-16.

This book, *"Maintaining Order In the church"* clearly expresses the heart of God to the Church regarding an area mostly neglected, yet of utmost importance if we are to see a triumphant Church emerge in these end times.

I am proud to say that the author, Lanre Sobo is to me what Timothy was to Paul. He progressively grew as a young convert in my ministry to become the Head Usher, Protocol Officer, Armor Bearer and then an ordained Minister. One statement I never heard him utter to me unlike others, was, *"Pastor, it cannot be done."*

As a matter of fact, though now separated by thousand of miles, he still serves in the capacity of Armor Bearer to me. His shoes in my ministry have been most difficult to fill neither has his competence been equaled and/or exceeded. This is to let the reader know that you have in your hands a book from an authoritative source.

This book is practical and pragmatic, based on experiential knowledge. It is a training manual that should be adopted by every Church or Ministry that desires to see order and excellence operating in whatever God has called her to do. I have seen the principles enumerated by the author work through his exemplary leadership, and I have no doubt that they will work for your team if they are taught to diligently practice them.

I must commend Lanre for blessing the Body of Christ with this timely book. If we avail ourselves of this great opportunity and digest the contents of the book, the knowledge acquired will save us from perishing (*Hosea 4: 6*), and will take the work of the Master in our hands from glory to glory.

God bless you as you help the Church of our Lord Jesus Christ soar like the eagle through the use of this must read book – "**Maintaining Order in the Church**"

Leke Sanusi
Pastor, RCCG, Victory House, London

PRESENTATION - 1

I am highly honored to present to you, *"Maintaining Order in the Church"* – a priceless gem written by one of my committed sons in the Lord. If there is any ministry of the church that is taken for granted, and yet is formidable, it is the Ushering Ministry.

Several, church growth efforts have suffered as a result of the positioning of square pegs in round holes and consequently, many Pastors have been short-changed despite their diligence and hard work. While the book addresses decency and order in the Church, it intelligently instructs its readers on the roles of the Usher, Protocol Officers and Armor Bearer.

The author in this book impresses upon his reader the fact that *"……..maintaining order in the Church is not merely a physical exercise, but also an activity in the spirit."* The role of the Holy Spirit in service is a veritable truth that provides needed balance for this wonderful work.

In conclusion, having been known all over the world as *"a stickler for excellence"*, it is my pleasure to present this excellent book as a deep reference material for both old and new comers to this ministry. God Bless you

Brown Oyitso
Provincial Pastor, RCCG, Nigeria

PRESENTATION - 2

The author has used his wealth of experience to shed some light upon subject matters that the Church has contributed little or no written resources to. If there is any arm of the Church that lacks sufficient documented resources, it is the Ministries of the Usher, Protocol Officer and Armor Bearer. When compared to other subject matters in the Church the scanty materials available on this subject pale in significance. The author has therefore done a wonderful job in painstakingly treating this important subject.

No business organization presents untrained, ill-equipped, and untested front office personnel to the public, yet the Church does this. The Ushering Department is the gateway or front office of the Church. Whatever impressions people form in their interactions with Ushers usually is a lasting one. Many visitors have vowed never to return to worship in certain Churches because of their gory experiences in the hands of untrained or ill-equipped Ushers. It would take only God to wipe out those impressions.

Have we considered the crude welcome treatment some Protocol Officers have on occasion given to visiting men of God? Or the way some visiting Ministers are kept waiting at airports, hotel lobbies or given bad reception because the Protocol team lacks proper etiquette. This shoddy treatment is quite common, and requires a lot of wisdom and expertise to correct, in order to minimize the negative consequences.

Consider also the Armor Bearers who in manifesting zeal without a proper understanding of their job description, end up carrying out several activities other than Armor Bearing? What is the role of the Holy Spirit in the Ministries of the Usher, Protocol Officer and Armor Bearer? How much of the work is being done in the flesh? Please know that whatever you lack in training cannot be replaced with raw or rugged ability. The thoughts intelligently addressed in this book are written from the author's personal experience in the field, and he sincerely seeks to impart them to others.

I therefore without any reservations present to you *"Maintaining Order in the Church"* as a must read not only for Ushers, Protocol Officers and Armor Bearers but also for those who want to appreciate this service in the House of God. God bless you all.

Taiwo Olusegun Ayeni
Rehoboth Bible Ministries Inc
Arlington, Texas.
www.rehobothbministries.org

PRESENTATION - 3

Apostle Paul instructs that we should *"let all things be done decently and in order"* because the default setting for any community is disorderliness. The church as a community of faith is not exempt from this disorderliness. Even though orderliness in the society is maintained by laws and their enforcement, but order in the church can only be maintained when our relationship with God goes beyond all legalism. Order will be maintained in the church when the church focuses on the commission to make disciples disciplined followers of Christ.

This book is a reflective testimony of someone who has passed through the way of God's call to the Ushering ministry. It is the intention of the author to pass a message of decency and order to the local church. It is a call to build men that can promote order in the midst of the universal disorderliness that the author has observed to have become the bane of the church.

In recommending this book and commending the author for lending his voice to a contemporary challenge, it is my hope that this work will provoke the church to rather engage in adaptive work instead of a technical or quick fix endeavor. As the author has affirmed, if you jump up, you will come down but when you grow up, you will stay up. Growth brings order while jumping creates disorderliness yet no one can legislate against jumping when children are in the house.

God bless you as you read this much-needed book.

Biodun Coker
Zonal Coordinator, RCCG, NA Zone 10
Dallas/Forth Worth Metroplex, USA.

PREFACE

Dear reader, please note that every account written in this book is a record of personal experiences and/or actions taken in the Church of God since my contact with the Lord.

In the course of my walk with the Lord, I realized a few years ago that a book like this should be written. This book is a reflective testimony of a life of active duty in response to God's call to service. The ideas detailed in this book have been successfully put to work while serving under seasoned servants of God, and acquiring various experiences that formed the bedrock of this work.

It is a privilege to be asked by the Lord to teach His people about *"Maintaining Order in the Church"*, and in a few chapters, this book addresses certain errors committed by God's children while providing various services in the local church. A message of decency and order is also taught here on how church proceedings should be carried out. Our Father who is the Judge of the Church has certain expectations, and they must be met.

The role, job specification and function of the Usher are addressed here for example the "front office" role of the church which the Usher plays and how very often it impacts the success of the Church in retaining new comers. This cannot be overemphasized. The roles, job specifications and functions of Greeters, Protocol Officers, and Armor Bearers are also examined with emphasis on the value of these offices to the Church. The importance of these offices are also enumerated, and briefly defined to give new comers into the Ministry a good foundation. Many have undermined the importance or significance attached to these Ministries out of ignorance and consequently believes there is no skill or training required in serving in these roles.

It is also important to understand that maintaining order in the Church is not merely a physical exercise, but also an activity in the spirit. An

Usher, Armor Bearer or Protocol Officer being an instrument in God's hand must maintain a close walk with God in prayer, possessing the ability to discern spiritual matters. So much is required of them if they must discharge their duties in maintaining order in the Church of God.

Who is this book for? If you are in any area of leadership or an active member in your Church or Fellowship, this book will sensitize you to the leading of Holy Spirit on how to apply the wisdom of God in every situation. While specifically focusing on Ushers, Protocol Officers, Greeters, and Armor Bearers, it is not limited to them. My prayer is that as you read this book, the Lord will cause a holy anger to rise up within you in order to resist and confront any form of misconduct in the Church of God, provoking and enabling you to overcome. I pray for an everlasting victory that will earn you a crown of honor on account of your service to God. Amen

✠ ✠ ✠

Chapter One

THE CALL

Our call, by the Lord Jesus Christ is to serve, and service in God's house is a commission that must be taken with all seriousness. The desire of God is for every man/ woman to follow after the pattern of the Lord who works while it is yet day. The harvest is truly plenteous but laborers are few, and this is the reason why they are being sought for to work in the Lord's vineyard. The vineyard of the Lord requires men/women who are diligent, faithful, and obedient to God's divine call.

The Bible declares in **John 5: 16** that, *"I have called you and ordained you"*. His call and ordination is for men in issues that pertain to Him,

1

and we are to respond to the needs of men and fulfill God's divine purpose. As partakers of His grace, we are to help the lost and lead the weary in the ways of the Lord. While we dutifully serve we must also lift up the hands of the Moses we have been called to follow, that the work of God should not suffer.

The importance of the work and the need for continuity of service is taught in **Matthew 28: 19-20** as the Lord Jesus was departing to be with the Father:

> *"Go therefore" and make disciples of all nations, baptizing them in the name of the Father and the son and of the Holy Spirit, teaching them to observe all things that I have commanded you; and lo, I am with you always, even to the end of age."*

I want to emphasize that the word **"Go"** is a word of command to you and I in His church; a command given to carry out certain duties. Unfortunately, the present Church seems to regard this command of Christ lightly and actions are being taken carelessly.

Over the years, I have observed the various ways Christians treat the things of God with carelessness but surprisingly, this casual behavior is limited to Church activities. This conduct is not exhibited in their respective secular jobs. What is the implication of this? It simply means that the children of God are treating with levity the institution created and commissioned by the sacrificial death and resurrection of our Lord Jesus Christ.

A man does not see anything wrong in walking into the church casually on a Wednesday or Sunday service after the opening prayer has been said. Others may even prefer to come just in time for the sermon so that they would not have to wait in church for too long. *Has the Church now become a place too inconvenient for God's children to visit?* When we set a time of 8.00am for a service or a conference, know for sure that God Himself is prepared and must of a necessity be there. The Bible says He is the controller of times and seasons and so our God is waiting for His children to be there at whatever time is stated.

In most cases however, what we usually have are just a few people in the sanctuary at the appointed time. You see others trooping in one by one, and by so doing are distractions to those others already in the presence of the Lord. While it makes sense for them to find the nearest available seats without causing any distraction, you find them trying to squeeze themselves into seats they find more convenient. The purpose of this is to have quick access to the Sanctuary exit anytime they choose to leave, whether or not the grace has been said or not. It is important to mention that this attitude is not limited to members alone, as some leaders (Workers, Ministers, and even Pastors) exhibit this trait too.

For example, we have a peculiar service every Friday in my local church that starts at 5.00 am called **"Good Morning Jesus."** Over the years that I have been attending this life transforming program, I have noticed with shock that a set of people unfailingly exhibit what I call a "set time arrival syndrome". It seems they have been programmed to arrive within a "set time". While the faithful ones arrive on or before 5.00 am, these other groups come in at 5:15am, 5:30am and 5:45am. I have monitored them over time with such consistency that when any of these groups mentioned come in for the service; I can accurately tell the time without checking my time piece. What a shame on these disrespectful people who have refused to be subject to the things of the Spirit.

The latter part of the above scripture states *"....teaching them to observe all things that I have commanded."* Our Lord Jesus Christ is concerned about having men taught all things that pertain to the kingdom of God. He desires that we have the balanced Word of God to make us grow as true disciples of His. His instructions therefore to those that had been with Him throughout His ministry were for them to teach others about Law and Order in His Church. If we all adhere to the biblical principles we are taught, both our spiritual and secular lives would be set in order.

The honest question before you now is, *"Is there Order in your church?"* The Lord is calling you today to obedience to His word and to the implementation of order in His house. He said *"...lo, I will be with you always even to the end of the age."* You need to start putting things in order in your Church because He is coming soon. When you obey Him, He is able to back you up till the end of time no matter what your situation is.

Furthermore, there is a clear instruction through Apostle Paul by the power of the Holy Spirit in 1Corinthians 14 verse 40:

> *"Let all things be done decently and in order."*

God is always interested in order in whatever venture we engage in. Paul told Timothy to set things in order in the Church and commanded him to appoint officers that would help him achieve this divine goal. The sheep must have shepherds and other leaders who would lift up "the hands of their Moses" in the Church Service in order for ministry to reach the grass root with no one left out.

The desire of God is to see His people carry out His instruction without wavering under any circumstance, and also becoming instruments of blessings to His sheep. While God is interested in the Church, He is also concerned about order in the nation. The period of King Saul's reign had produced disorder in the land. Everything was on the decline and God was so unhappy with the king that He began to shop for another king in David. He therefore gave a clear directive to Prophet Samuel towards attaining this set objective in 1Samuel 16: 1:

> *"Fill your horn with oil, and go; I am sending you to Jesse the Bethlehemite. For I have provided Myself a King among his sons."*

God is the one that has called you and not for a moment should you think it is the Pastor or

Minister who has appointed you to the position of maintaining order in His house. He will surely give guidance in effecting this calling. Samuel nearly made a mistake in choosing a wrong king for Israel and you can imagine what this should have bought upon Israel and its people. The error of judgment would have resulted in a wrong king, wrong order, and wrong judgment, but we thank God that the Strength of Israel who cannot lie came to the scene in time. He that is never late took up the gauntlet and intervened to rescue the nation from a potential disaster.

The Master Himself puts things in order and through the help of the Holy Spirit guided Prophet Samuel to make the right choice. If you find yourself in such a situation and you need to make a crucial decision for your church, I believe the God of decency and order will make a way out for you in Jesus name. Amen. My confidence is that God is with you all the way, and He will not allow you to fail.

May be for one reason or the other you are saying to yourself *"Am I qualified to act in this capacity?"* The answer is *"Yes"*. God is interested in people you least expect to do anything in His house. David in that chapter was least expected of the sons of Jesse to be king but God fished him out of the bush.

I have found in my time in ministry that people that put things in order in church or enforce discipline in the Church are those who have been involved in similar situations when they were in the world as unbelievers. Some were notorious and very obedient to the world. For example people who have been involved in secret cults, social clubs, secret organizations etc. and whom God has saved are often used by the Holy Spirit to channel the same effort and passion they had used in serving Satan to serve God in keeping order.

If you are wondering right now whether I used to be an ex member of any of these organizations, the answer is *"Yes"*. I was very concerned about perfection when I was an active member of a social club in my university days, and God has turned that same zeal towards the affairs of His Church. He did not take that gift away from me but remolded it and used it to reshape my destiny.

An Associate Pastor in London, England happened to be a Chief Commandant in a secret cult society when he was in the university. He was an expert at keeping order in kingdom of Satan but God touched his life, saved him and he is currently Administrator of the Church he attends. The public testimony of the Pastor-In–charge of that Church at a conference is that he the Pastor does not run his church. All he does is to communicate the vision, and this Associate Pastor carries out the execution of such vision. What a great testimony. Can the same be testified about you?

The call of God is unique and sometimes we wonder how he singles a person out from the crowd and puts his anointing upon that person. I remember arriving in London, England many years ago in the heat of summer, and life seemed so good after having escaped the hardship of my home country. I was a casual churchgoer and I did not want to associate with any Church that would make demands on me. In fact, I located a Church from a denomination I had never attended before because I liked the service. Why? Because it lasted about an hour and all I needed to do was walk in casually just in time for the message and quickly leave after service. I thought I was at least doing some thing right by going to Church, as my peers did not even take Church so seriously. I actually thought I was on the Lord's side - foolish me. This is exactly what the Lord calls self-righteousness.

No one in that Church called me to order and I suffered greatly in hands of the Devil as I kept treating the affairs of God and His Church lightly. I however thank God for saving and delivering me from the kingdom of darkness and transporting me into His glorious light. He engineered this process through my wife Kemi, (then my fiancé) whom God miraculously relocated from Nigeria to London, England and who forcefully took me and introduced me to The Redeemed Christian Church of God (RCCG) where I was saved and finally delivered.

After a few months in the Church, the Holy Spirit began to work in me and I discovered that my first primary assignment in the Church is to restore order. What a marvelous God we serve!

✠ ✠ ✠

Chapter Two

ARE YOU EQUIPPED?

One of the greatest challenges faced in Ministry of today is the fact that many who are "called" are quite ready to occupy positions of high visibility in the church but are not prepared to undergo training. This brings adverse consequences in the functioning and operations of many churches. The kingdom of darkness is aware of this, and feels comfortable even when we have successfully won souls into the kingdom. He knows assuredly well that these new converts in the hands of untrained workers will soon take a u-turn and return to their vomit.

Lack of training has affected the effective handling of souls won during evangelism and other outreach programs of the church. Some baby Christians have been put off by untrained and unskilled workers, who lack refined method of handling newcomers to the house of God. Some are not received with affection; or are treated crudely, and/or never followed up. Church members make matters worse by not showing interest, or sharing love with visitors after the church service. In some situations after the usual welcome pep talk, and prayer they are left hanging around, looking embarrassed, isolated, ostracized and hoping someone may at least come to their rescue while they wait for the ones who brought them to church.

Cases like these have brought untold embarrassment to the body of Christ. We have through our untrained hands sent willing souls back to the alluring arms of the world, to continue in their sins to the fullest while we wonder why? How many times have we seen people stop going to church just because of what fellow believers did or did not do? Some accounts are too terrible to be put in print.

This seems to be a common problem with many churches of God, and is one of the reasons for the high turnover of new people visiting the churches. Unless the Workers, Ministers and Pastors are trained to meet the diverse needs of people who are hungry for relevance, welcome and love, the church still has a problem in her hands.

In this chapter, we want to lay adequate emphasis on training in relation to maintaining order in the church. Issues like "Why do I need training?" "The relevance of training", "Why people don't get adequate training'" and "The effects of training on the church" etc. are to be examined. We must not forget that; *"You cannot give what you don't have."* This is one of the simple reasons why this book is placed in your hands.

TRAINING

What is training? To train means to *"sharpen"* or *"make ready, sound, whole, complete, and healthy for every good work"*. The book of *Psalm 119: 80* says: *"Let my heart be sound in thy statutes; that I be not ashamed"*

There are several types of training:

- Life long Training: This is borne out of life's experiences acquired as one passes through the various stages of life. Experience they say is a better teacher. The setting for this kind of training is the world.

- Short and long term hands-on (on the job) training or mentoring. Learning by watching what others are doing, asking question and having the opportunity to practice them on site.

- Classroom setting training, Seminars, Conferences or training workshops.

- On-line Internet based training and/or correspondence by mail trainings.

- Personal training through deliberate acquisition of information e.g. books, bulletins, magazines, journals, tapes, CD's etc to improve ones self over time due to observed or perceived inadequacy, self training on the web, interviewing people, collecting and collating materials

However, in the service of God there are certain things training cannot replace, as it is only a tool to enhance what is already made available. For example:

- Training cannot replace the work of the Holy Spirit

- Training can be formal and/or informal whereby one can be taught by observing what others do, but it cannot replace absence of grace to do the work.

- Training is not a substitute for motivation, commitment, and hard work, which enhance the effect of training.

REASONS PEOPLE ARE NOT TRAINED

Why are some people not trained? It could be for any one or more of the following reasons:

- They don't see the need for it

- They don't make time for it

- They don't cooperate with their trainers

- Not many trainers are prepared to make sacrifices.

- They are impatient to graduate

Workers or Ministers who sometimes maintain order in a local church have often deprived themselves of the training available because they believe they do not need it. They erroneously believe that God's work does not require such high or detailed standard that are required in secular organizations. Consequently, they take self-development in the service of God's work for granted, and carry out their duties the way they deem fit, not the way it ought to be properly done. *Matthew 9: 35-38* gives us an understanding of this problem.

> *"But when He saw the multitudes, He was moved with compassion on them, because they fainted, and were scattered abroad, as sheep having no Shepherd. Then saith He unto His disciples, the harvest truly is plenteous, but the laborers are few; Pray ye therefore the Lord of the harvest, that He will send forth laborers into His harvest."*

We see that even though the harvest is truly plenteous the laborers are few because many people are unwilling to commit themselves to labor in God's vineyard. Even with those who have willingly offered to serve, there is only a few that are really trained and equipped to carry on the work. This is the reason why we have inefficient Workers in our churches, and this conversely impacts and affects the work.

It is so important that the church channels its efforts to train the brethren who have manifested certain elements of grace or calling for the work as we read in 1Peter 4: 10

> *"As every man hath received the gift, even so minister the same one to another, as good stewards of the manifold grace of God."*

Research has shown that a good number of our people lack adequate understanding about how the work of God ought to be done. Others conclude that satanic distractions and procrastination are responsible for the inefficient administration of order in our churches. I would also want to add that the church leadership sometimes does not pass across adequate information on the nature and dimensions of the work, painting the picture half way and then expecting so much from the sheepfold.

Remember Jesus Christ would tell His disciples parables, ask them what it meant, and then later explain its meaning by breaking it down to His disciples with simpler articulation. He did not assume they knew, but always endeavored to teach them as one having authority. This quality sometimes is lacking in some of our leaders.

Sometimes, the fact that Workers are not aware of the actual rewards that follow their commitment and service to God not only hampers their performance but also robs them of their blessing. Detailed teachings should always emphasize the rewards of following and the consequences of denying Him. This would help them to know where to cast their net, and be a blessing in God's house as they serve in all diligence. For example, Peter asked the Lord about the reward he would get for following Him. The Master did not mince words about the blessings that await him and others who choose to follow Him.

May be someone is asking this question; "Why do I need training?" It is because God wants excellence and order in the church and He emphasized this by making it a requirement in the Holy Bible. Elisha, Moses, Apostles Paul, Barnabas, Timothy etc were all trained. Working in the kingdom of God or the church requires special skills which training sharpens by impacting knowledge, gift development, and character alignment. It is also necessary to appreciate the fact that God's standards are very high. God said so much about this in Daniel 5: 12 using Daniel as a point in reference:

> *"Forasmuch as an excellent Spirit, and knowledge, and understanding, interpreting of dreams, and showing of hard sentences, dissolving of doubts, were found in same Daniel, whom the king named Belteshazzar: now let Daniel be called, and he will show the interpretation."*

Daniel and all his friends were no pushovers. They were trained in one of the best institutions of learning in Babylon and the book of Daniel Chapter one gives insight about this. Moses was trained in the courts of Pharaoh and raised to be a leader of men. He advanced his training through practical exposure as a shepherd of his father-in-law's sheep. Paul the Apostles was effectively taught under the scholarly guidance of Gamaliel, a notable teacher of the law and letters.

It is important to know that God wants us to be trained because He wants us to maintain proper order in our handling of and involvement in the souls of men. Those in authority cannot afford to be careless because you might be the only hope for that soul. This is the reason the bible enjoins us in Ecclesiastes 9: 10 that:

"Whatsoever thy hand findeth to do, do it with thy might; for there is no work, nor device, nor knowledge, nor wisdom, in grave, whither thou goest".

While it is important to note that a lack of training results in an inability to effectively manage people, we must admit that not everyone is a training material. You can only train a man who has been endowed by God's grace and requires a little push to be able to stand, walk, and run. For example Eli had to train Samuel when God began a journey of fellowship with him and Samuel as at yet did not know that it was God calling him - I Samuel 3: 1-10.

A lot of the crisis and misconduct which we see in the church today will need extraordinary trained people to maintain order in such churches. There is nothing as dangerous as a half trained Worker. He is a time bomb waiting to explode, and when he does, he is going to wreak extensive havoc anywhere he detonates. Suffice it to say, it is better not to train a man than to expose him to improper and unfinished training. All you have succeeded in doing is wetting his appetite and giving him the impression that he is ready. We have situations like this in many of our churches, where half-baked, run-off-the-mill men and women are manning serious spiritual duty posts.

No intelligent management executive or military leader will assign improperly trained personnel, to hold sensitive positions within their organizations, yet we do this within the Body of Christ. These "90-day wonders" as they call them in the army continue to wreak untold havoc within the Body of Christ. I pray the Lord would open our eyes to see the need, and provide extensive training for our Ministers, Workers, Protocol Officers, Ushers, Choir members etc. May God help us as we strive to respond and make training efforts as from today in Jesus name, Amen.

✠ ✠ ✠

Chapter Three

WHO IS THAT USHER?

Shortly before I got delivered as a casual Christian I had a conviction that God was leading me into my destiny but it seemed so vague to me. The Bible says He is the beginning and the end, the author and finisher of our faith. God's original plan for my life was already prepared and, no matter how long I kept wandering, I sensed that He was about to finally lead me into my destiny.

I began to attend some popular Pentecostal churches and I noticed certain differences in their mode of operations and services as compared with the churches I had previously attended. On a particular visit I was aware of the way in which I was welcomed into the church, the warmth in the smile and the handshake of the Usher.

Upon entering the church my next experience was a different scenario entirely. I went my usual way, already determined in my mind where I would sit. I am aware that most casual Christians are guilty of this. While I wanted to look for the last and most convenient seat at the back of the auditorium, enabling me to easily dash out when necessary, it was so obvious that if I sat there, I would be the only one seated at the back of the sanctuary. The Ushers would not allow this, and they prevailed on me in a loving and friendly manner to change my seat. I had no choice but to do this because of their caring approach. Their warm demeanor broke the seed of rebellion within me and set me on the path of divine change, which I still traverse upon, till today.

These Ushers were very organized and firm in the way they sat people on the available pews as they come in and out of the church. There was no breaking of ranks at all as they seemed to know their job description very well. These efficient Workers were truly instruments in God's hands, worthy of emulation.

Still on my story, if I had insisted on my preferred seat and refused to go to where I was directed, my carnal action would have been obvious to other parishioners. Since I did not really want to be noticed, I went quietly and reluctantly to sit where I was directed. The spirit of disorder was brought under control; order was maintained despite my wrong motives. The result was obedience on my part and we all know that what follows obedience is blessing. I am convinced that I received a blessing that day because what I had never done before was recorded in my spiritual logbook.

Please note that I was called to "order", in the church by an Usher within a few minutes of entering the church and this is the way it ought to be. Not only must an Usher know his job description very well, he must be bold to execute it in love, not grudgingly. For example, calling a five hundred member congregation to order in the area of seating would make a difference in that service because distractions will ultimately affect the flow of the Holy Spirit during the service. God wants things done decently and in order and where it is maintained, you will find Him present.

Dear Ushers, please understand that you have major duty and part to play in the success of the service or program. The office of the Usher is a spiritual position and the responsibility must be spiritually discerned. Remember the feeding of the five thousand souls in *Matthew 14: 19*, Jesus commanded the multitudes to sit down on the grass. He maintained order to prepare the way for miracles. Now, this is a major determinant of God's visitation in a service and the truth that God acknowledges and honors such in His house. The issue of order was also addressed in detail in Paul's epistles to the Corinthians and to Titus. The first epistle to the Corinthians is devoted to dealing with maintaining order in the Church, especially in *Chapters 5 to 8*. In *Titus 1: 5* Paul said:

"For this cause left I thee in Crete, that thou shouldest set in order the things that are wanting, …..".

If order, is expected to be maintained in church, and Paul left Titus behind for this purpose, then Ushers should see themselves as part of this charge as collaborators in advancing the work of God, and moving it to higher grounds.

Many ushers in the church take their positions lightly, not acknowledging the fact that they are as important in ensuring God's move in the lives of the people during the service as the Minister preaching the gospel. When God distributed callings or ministry gifts, He did not isolate the Ministry of helps, from pastoral, apostolic, teaching, evangelistic, and the prophetic. No! Everyone is supposed to collaborate with one another and not compete. God regards all of these as spiritual callings and attaches to them spiritual gifts that should enhance their performances in ministry.

The day I made the above statement as Head Usher, most of the other Ushers were shocked, but this truth invariably changed their perspective of the ministry. They now do not see themselves as just a bunch of people who shake hands and pass the offering bucket around the church but as Spirit led tools in the hand of God. In the next Chapter, we will take time to outline the role of an Usher in a local assembly, and the duties expected of them as they serve in the Lord's vineyard.

✠ ✠ ✠

Chapter Four

THE ROLE OF AN USHER

As mentioned in the earlier chapter, the role of an Usher is as crucial in any service as that of the Minister preaching the Word. However, some Ushers do not know this and hence they regard their positions lightly. Their refusal to acknowledge the fact that they are as important to ensure God's move in the lives of the people during that service as the Minister preaching the gospel has robbed both them, and the people they serve of certain crucial blessings required for growth in their Christian walk. The ministry of the Usher is to collaborate with other ministries and not to compete. Below is a briefly itemized list of roles, functions of and expectations from an Usher in any church setting.

i) Assists the Pastor: The Usher is expected to assist the Pastor as he ministers during the service, and a good example is when the offering is about to be taken. Have you been in a service when it is time to take an offering and you hear from the pulpit "Could we have someone to help?" I have been there before and I wondered what was going on in this disorganized setting. I also wondered what action the fellow who collected the offering would do take thereafter. Also to mention ushers who wear looks on their faces that indicates bankruptcy. However, there are procedures in the house of God for doing all things and the taking of the offering must likewise be carried out decently and in order.

Imagine if the Pastor calls for the offering and you have two to four Ushers promptly marching forward to provide assistance. What a great example of the ministry of helps at work. I recommend in any church no matter how small that at least two people should receive the offering. Under no circumstances should only one person pass the offering basket. This has to do with accountability and dependency. In the UK officials of the Charities Commission (the equivalent of the Internal Revenue Service of the U.S.) have been known to visit churches to observe how they collect offerings, maintain order and convey offerings collected to the treasury.

You would never know that these agents were present in your service until your administrator receives a letter of audit request. Most times this request is a major investigation because they have seen more than you could ever have imagined. It is therefore critical that Ushers maintain order and handle the affairs in the house of God with decency and order. May the good Lord bless you as you do so.

ii) **Meets and Greets:** These Ushers are the public spokespersons of the church. Note that Pastors cannot greet everybody. They are the first point of contact with all the guests and existing members of the church and are the front office of the church. They are to maintain the best smiles and manners ever seen in a person, not mechanical ones, but smiles with warmth which flows from within because *"in the presence of the Lord is the fullness of joy"*.

They should also be smartly dressed, tidy and maintain clean breath. A guest usually decides within a moment of contact with the Greeter of a church if he or she is going to return to the church or not. From the welcome, handshake, smile, passing of the church bulletin, escort to the seats, final welcome, sermon, announcements etc., impressions are being created and each activity is a process leading to a vital decision.

Very serious concern and attention should be given to people who serve in this capacity because their actions can either be detrimental or positive to the church. If an Usher oozes with a bad body odor, it would take the grace of God for any visitor who has had a close contact with this Usher to return to the Church. The visitor, even when he thinks of a revisit would probably be imagining in his heart *"Will that Usher be at the door again this morning?"* This in itself is a discouraging thought that would never have arisen if the Usher has taken good care of him or her self. First impressions are so vital.

The Usher with a rough attitude would repel people from the church. This attitude is counterproductive in the ministry and such Ushers must be advised to submit themselves to training. Two ladies came to testify of their experiences on a certain Sunday. The first lady stated how she was heavy hearted and burdened that Sunday morning and was not in the mood to go to church. While she was thinking of her problems, she remembered the smiling face of the Greeter in the church, and was immediately encouraged. She dashed into her room, put her dress on in a hurry and drove to church. As soon as she expectantly got to church, guess whom she met at the door? It was the smiling Usher.

The second lady indicated that she and her children were church hunting and scouting for a home church. Their search was completely over when they met the smiling Usher at the entrance of the gate. To them there was no need to search anymore and they made up their minds within few minutes of this encounter that they had found a home church. It was not long before she joined the same Ushering team, and she is presently playing an active role as a Greeter in the same church.

iii) **Maintains Order**. A Pastor made reference in one of his books to how he was beaten up on Sunday morning service by an unruly man. This man kept making side comments during the sermon and the Ushers were not very alert to either caution him or quell the disturbance.

When the Pastor noticed what was going on, he confronted the man and sought to maintain order. Unfortunately for the Pastor, he made a statement that incited the anger of the unruly man and the result was a nasty scene in the church on a Sunday morning. Now, where were the Ushers?

It is always advisable for any Ushering team to have Ushers with designated roles e.g. to keep such people out of the service and also protect the Pastor, guest Ministers or any other person handling any pulpit ministration. The nature of the roles would of course depend upon the resources and manpower available.

I remember a striking incident that could again very easily occur whenever any Pastor is at the pulpit. A lady dressed as minister of the gospel with a round collar band across her neck walked into the service and I immediately sensed uneasiness in the spiritual atmosphere. The lady approached the altar just like everybody but I had a witness to be alert and stay directly on guard for the Pastor. I obeyed and I observed that the Pastor himself felt very uncomfortable during the approach of this lady. As I stood firm gazing into the eyes of the woman indicating a "no access" stand concerning her approach to the Pastor, order was enforced in the service. She stopped in her tracks, turned back, and grudgingly walked away.

At the end of the service, the Pastor came, shook my hand, and said "Well done!" He explained that certain spirits attempt to test the power of God and the sensitivity of God's children. Thank God I acted promptly otherwise the consequences could have been like that of the Pastor I mentioned earlier or even worse. This was an even more direct spiritual attack. Ushers be on guard as you maintain order in the church.

The question before every Usher is, *"Are you gifted for this call?"* or *"Are you trained and cultured for the role you are playing?"* or *"Did you join the Ushering department to be noticed or to serve?"* This minute or moment pause and have a rethink about your service in God's house.

May I briefly share with you my story? My very first assignment in the house of God was to be an Usher. As soon as I identified and realized this calling, I availed myself of all <u>relevant training existing</u> in the church in order to be equipped for service. I did not take the role casually, because I recognized that it was a spiritual calling requiring spiritual execution.

I understood that my actions would influence other believers and visitors as I remembered my personal experience with the Ushers that attended to me in the past. If you recall, I earlier wrote *"Their warm demeanor broke the seed of rebellion within me and set me on the path of divine change, which I still traverse upon, till today"*. Ushers, you must remember that you are the front office personnel of the Church, inviting or repelling people either by your action or inaction.

On my first day in service as an Usher, I had zealously fasted as I had been briefed earlier that prayer and fasting was paramount every Sunday for all Workers in the church. As I welcomed people into the church with a good smile, a lady walked in and snapped at me. This startled me, as I was shocked to behold such an unbecoming behavior from a believer. Her response clearly indicated to me that she did not want to be directed to a seat and had already selected her seat.

Trust Satan, he brought my attention back to the times I had personally done the same thing but thank God for the Holy Spirit who also reminded me that if I could change she also could. The way she confronted me was very aggressive and after I let her take the seat she wanted, I said to myself that all I could do was to pray harder so that the other guests would not behave badly like that lady.

I continued with my duties and prayed for the lady asking God to have mercy on her because she was out of order. To my surprise God proved to me that He hears and answer prayers. After the service, the lady came to me and apologized. She told me she was disobedient, felt very uncomfortable throughout the service but now she felt very good with herself now that she had apologized. God does answer prayers and sometimes they come instantly.

This is a lesson to Ushers who meet quite a few uncooperative people when they come into the church. Don't get annoyed and/or create a scene, keep praying for the touch of God. One of my fellow Ushers would in the past run to me anytime someone confronted her, expecting me to take up action with such person. I always said to her from experience that it is better handled with prayer than confrontation, which sometimes generates friction rather than resolution. The following itemized areas should be the concern of ushers:

a) Prayer: This should be an added inspiration for every Usher because we deal with both the spiritual and unspiritual people who wake up on the very bad side of their beds before coming to church. We deal with some unruly people who can only be touched not by the power <u>of our experience</u> as Ushers but by the power of prayer through grace that issues from God's divine presence.

b) Decency: Other area that should concern us is the aspect of decency. Every indecent attitude noticed during service should be handled with wisdom. For example, when you notice someone making side comments when the Pastor is preaching and creating an atmosphere that can grieve the Holy Spirit; you need to wisely step in and maintain order. As a bold and wise Usher you take charge of this, by correcting them with a lovely smile but still passing the message across.

c) Sitting Arrangement: Another thing you must observe, as an Usher is never to sit any indecently dressed lady (especially with a mini skirt) in the front row, whether or not she is a visitor. This kind of seating arrangement brings distraction to those sitting at the altar or ministering from the pulpit and can affect the move of the Holy

Spirit. You must be sensitive enough to know whom you sit in the first row in church. Pray to God to give you the grace to discern and endow you with discretion.

Where there is no crèche for the babies, it is very important never to sit nursing mothers with babies on the same row and/or close to one another. This is because the bonding that quickly takes place will lead to another service within the service. It is necessary that you map out strategies to sit them in such a way that they are not too close to each other. Nursing mothers that sit together are bound to start a chat during service.

d) Maintain Eye Contact: A very important tool in Ushering is the "Eye Contact Rule" I train ushers to use this principle as it limits distraction, less movement and maintains smooth coordination during service. It might not be an ideal strategy depending on the size of the church but if carried out effectively, it works.

When you notice excessive movements during a church service, it is sometimes an indication of inadequate preparation. Ushers can avoid moving from one point to another during a service by using the Eye Contact Rule effectively if they are well positioned. If you notice a disturbance at a location distant from you and have another Usher who is relatively nearer, rather than walking all that way, it will only take an eye contact to get the attention of that usher to deal with the situation. While Ushers are on the alert keeping watch on everyone, they should also maintain close eye contact frequently. A negative or positive nod from the head indicates action to be taken without traveling across the auditorium.

e) Duty Post Exchange: This is a systematic way Ushers take turns for a particular assignment that requires more than one Usher. The rule is never to leave your duty post until your relief Usher gets near or by you. This rule is also very relevant to those Ushers designated to stand in front of the church especially during the sermon or when the Senior Pastor or guest Pastor is on the pulpit. This is a very sensitive post and must be spiritually attended to. The primary duty of this Usher is not to attend to the needs of parishioners but to keep guard and maintain order in that section of the church. A soldier would never leave his or her duty post without a replacement. The consequences are severe if he acts otherwise. This principle applies in the church, and a vacuum created by an Usher can result in disorder during the service.

Some Ushering teams use the Eye Contact Rule or scheduled time slots to exchange posts. I can confidently say this brings order in the church and the Ushering team gains a lot of respect and confidence from Pastors, ministers, and even the parishioners. In essence, Ushers must be alert and sensitive in the spirit. This tells God that His people are ready for His attention to be manifested.

✠ ✠ ✠

Chapter Five

THE ARMOR BEARER

The word Armor Bearer was widely used in the Old Testament as in the instances of Saul, Jonathan, and David. In fact, we see how when Saul died how his Armor Bearer fell on his sword, and died with his master:

"And when his Armor Bearer saw that Saul was dead, he fell likewise upon his sword, and died with him" 1Samuel 31: 5.

The Armor Bearer's role is to be all things to his Lord, as they are one in the service. The failure of the Armor Bearer's service may impact the ministry of his master. See for example the role of Jonathan's Armor Bearer and his submission to his master when he informed him about God's leading. This was a time in Israel where nobody but Saul and Jonathan had swords, shield and spears in the land, yet the Armor Bearer with weapons of war was willing to risk his life and obey divine leading (1Samuel 13: 19-22.) In 1Samuel 14: 6–7 we read:

> *"And Jonathan said unto the young man that bare his armor, Come, and let us go over unto the garrison of these uncircumcised; it may be that the Lord will work for us: for there is no restraint to the Lord to save by many or by few. And his Armor Bearer said unto him, Do all that is in thine heart; turn thee behold, I am with thee according to thy heart".*

Jonathan being touched of God to carry out a risky assignment shared it with the young man, and his response was that of willingness to follow the counsel of the Lord, An Armor Bearer should be an ardent follower, following his master as he in turn follows Jesus. If you take time to read the story, you will see how God through both Jonathan and his Armor Bearer wrought miracles for

Israel, and delivered the nation from the hands of the Philistines.

"So the Lord saved Israel that day: and the battle passed over unto Beth-aven" - 1Samuel 14: 23.

Who did God use to save Israel? It was the obedient Jonathan, and his Armor Bearer. The Armor Bearer as a subordinate or follower must be willing to lay down his life where necessary, fighting the battles together and rejoicing when victory comes. He has the responsibility of bearing the armor of his superior officer. In fact you can refer to him as a servant, dedicated to service.

In the New Testament, the word armor bearer is synonymous with discipleship. The word disciple was popularly used back then, but in real sense they both refer to service to others. As mentioned earlier, he is someone who is willing to lay down his life or sacrifice all for another in the course of fulfilling his call to service. One may not see himself as one, but a closer look at the scripture reveals this fact. If the disciple of our Lord Jesus did all in order for the gospel to be preached all over the world, with the sacrifices of time, family, friend and even lives, one can invariably conclude that these were indeed Armor Bearers of our Lord

Jesus Christ, and the ambassadors of the kingdom of God.

On that note I will conclude that any child of God, follower of our Lord Jesus Christ and promoter of the gospel is an Armor Bearer, one who defends, maintains order in the church, neighborhood, community, city, and the nation at large. Pastors especially need people who are reliable around them. They prayerfully select leaders within the church that are closest to them because the quality of the Pastor's leadership is a function of the quality of people around him or his Armor Bearers. The officer on whom the king leaned on was also a **Lord**, that is, a leader in his own right - *2Kings 7: 2.* Let us briefly look at few people that bore the armor of their leaders:

Joseph served Pharaoh and his own generation, and his contributions preserved lives in nations. It all started with one visit to the king's palace - *Genesis 41: 38-40.*

A good example is the case of Aaron and Hur who lifted the hands of Moses to ensure total victory on the mount. Many may remember Aaron more for his error but he was still the only one who could fill the national vacuum created when Moses stayed on the mountain for forty days

- *Exodus 32: 1.* Imagine the church without a Pastor or leader for just a few weeks.

Daniel served different kings beginning from King Nebuchadnezzar. He was a choice leader and the most outstanding of three top leaders in the kingdom of Media and Persia - *Daniel 6: 2.*

Elisha, a young farmer turned out to be a world-class leader. In modern day terms he will be known as "die hard" He followed after Elijah the prophet and beyond pouring water on his masters' hands, he became his successor - *2King 2: 15.* These are references from the book "**Lean on me**" by Steve Akoni.

My Pastor officially drafted me into this ministry some years back, and I thought within myself that my service as an Usher had equipped me to have all I needed to know to maintain order in the house of God. However as months and years rolled forward I saw that the ministry was more demanding, and required more commitment than I realized. The job description challenges your every day activities, and the motto of the ministry of an Armor Bearer is "**all things are possible...**"

This call increased my visibility because I was bearing the armor of the Senior Pastor. The level of accessibility to the man of God increased, and everything concerning him, his ministry, family, activities etc was my responsibility to protect by bearing his armor. As I grew in this ministry, I found out that protecting the man of God, his entire endeavors etc. formed part of my role of protecting the church of God and maintaining order in it.

I will outline some qualities and duties of an Armor Bearer, relate personal experiences, and help you to discover how you can position yourself effectively to fulfill this role. Remember as an ambassador of Christ you carry the armor of the gospel, and nothing must tarnish or bring disorder to the things of God.

i) **Spirit of Excellence:** Daniel had the spirit of excellence and there was an account about this man that there was no person like him in the entire land. Many kings sought after him because of his right attitude and the spirit in him. To be an Armor Bearer you must attain and maintain consistent high standards. Please note that excellence is different from perfection that terminates when attained. Excellence is evolving and so you keep breaking your own records. There is a saying and I quote "**Man's worse enemy of progress is not the people around him but his last achievements.**" This is because he could decide that after finishing this beautiful work he will take a break. This is not an option for the Armor Bearer who desires to maintain order in the church. You keep striving towards excellence, never getting tired but instead receiving grace to refire.

ii) Consistency: This quality is essential for an Armor Bearer. I was tested in this very manner for several years. Any Pastor will test your commitment over time before giving you the latitude to make your full impact felt.

iii) Skills: David was a very skillful man as we read 1Samuel 16: 18:

> *"Then answered one of the servants, and said behold, I have seen a son of Jesse the Bethlehemite, that is cunning in playing, and a mighty valiant man, and a man of war, and prudent in matters, and a comely person, and the Lord is with him."*

Pastors need the professional skills of other gifted people to enhance their effectiveness. As I advanced in Information Technology skills, all I desired daily was to bring new ideas to the church and enhance the ministry of my Pastor.

iv) Character: The common index of Christian character is the fruit of the Spirit - Galatians 5: 22-23. The key to spiritual growth of an Armor Bearer is in his character. See the example of Saul's Armor Bearer in 2 Samuel 14 when he refused to strike his leader in his time of weakness. What a loyal soldier! As an Armor Bearer one must be able to handle confidential matters especially the weaknesses of your leader.

v) Integrity: Integrity is crucial. I wish to quote from the book *"Lean on me"* by Steve Akoni on this subject:

> *"Reputation is different from integrity. It is great to have both but if you have not been so opportune, you seek to develop integrity. Some have reputation but not integrity. Charisma, through reputation can get position but without integrity you will not keep it for long."*

Bishop Dr. David Oyedepo of Living Faith World Outreach Center once said, *"If you jump up, you will come down, but when you grow up, you stay up"* I pray you will grow up if you find yourself in this ministry.

vi) Availability: When a man makes himself available he will be used because God is always looking for men and women who are available to serve. Once I heard a man of God addressing some of his members who always gave excuses of being busy whenever their services were needed in the church. They would always find one excuse or the other. This Pastor relieved the Workers of all their duties and told them to reapply whenever they had the time and could be available. It is very vital as Christians to pray concerning situations that might deter us from serving the Lord. Pray when you look for that secular job and be specific about your request.

The mistake we sometimes make as leaders is to try very hard to carry everybody along, thereby causing a lot dragging of the work in the church. This was a very hard decision for the Pastor to make, but he was able to streamline the team, identifying those who were ready to serve at that time and then making effective use of them. In Luke 14: 18-24 some people were given an opportunity to partake of God's goodness but were giving excuses. Those you least expected were available and were given the opportunity to serve. They carried away all the blessings. The Bible clearly informs us that God does not use idle but busy hands. For example, Elisha was farming when God called him to serve, Gideon was busy threshing wheat and Peter was struggling to catch fish.

vii) Holy Spirit: *The book of* Acts 6 verse 3 says - *"Wherefore, brethren, look ye out among you seven men of honest report, full of the Holy Spirit and wisdom, whom we appoint over this business.* As an Armor Bearer the anointing and power of the Holy Ghost must be manifested in your life because He must direct our affairs concerning the matters of the kingdom.

viii) Program Facilitator: As an Armor Bearer you have a responsibility to see to the success of every project or activity in the church / within the ministry. This includes all aspects of the project, from the simplest to the hardest. Essentially, an Armor Bearer ensures that things are in place without necessarily getting in the way of other Ministry/Workers. I would outline all the Ministries involved in that program, listing all the leaders in charge. Once the vision for the program is defined, I would make a random check with the leaders of those departments to see if everything was in place for the program.

Following up on their activities would not compromise their authority because all you are trying to do is to protect the interests of the church and the program. Your enquiries should be done with the intention to assist if there is a problem. Programs will often be successful if there are committed Armor Bearers to take the responsibility of ensuring the success of the programs. Taking care of little things prior to the day of the event always helps to avoid big problems. During programs when you see people running around you can tell that the organizers have been ill prepared.

As an Armor Bearer, one of the things that helped me to succeed as a program facilitator was visiting other programs. Apart from participating in the programs, I would take a close look at my surroundings, observing structures, procedures, and tools that were put in place especially for the program. I did not pick many ideas often but even the simplest ideas could be re-packaged and improved upon in your local church.

At a conference in London, a popular preacher much loved and admired for his gifting made a remarkable statement when asked from where he gets all his ideas. He told his audience that those ideas came from his attendance at the programs of Pastors of both small and large congregations. He further shocked the Pastors and Ministers present by adding that some of the big things they saw happening in his ministry were learnt from some of the smaller churches he attended as a Guest Minister. All he did was to repackage them.

This man of God saw himself as an Armor Bearer, learning how to perfect the things of God. I challenge you today to be sensitive to your environment, knowing that every little idea you observe can become bigger not only in your church but even in your personal life.

ix) **A Warrior:** A warrior is one who is called to fight e.g. a soldier, who does not entangle himself with civilian affairs, but endures hardness as a good soldier in the service of his master –2Timothy 2: 3-4. Such a person should be willing to render service, making his abilities available in order to ensure victory particularly in spiritual battles.

Everyday activities in the church involve warfare because the Devil is always contending with the progress of the church. Mathew 16: 18 says that:

"...upon this rock I will build my church and the gates of hell shall not prevail against it". This means that as the church advances, the Devil launches attacks in order to visit the church with disorder, but the Lord assures us that he will not prevail.

It is the duty of warriors to engage in warfare and ensure victory all times. Oftentimes even as an Armor Bearer, assignments are given by the Pastor at very inconvenient times, but because the intention of such was to bring order into the house of God, I made sure I carried out such assignments even if they will cost me sleepless nights. The joy you receive when you see God's glory manifested knows no bounds.

I remember vividly often receiving late evening calls from my Pastor with instructions about things he wanted ready, and in place for the Worship Service the following day. He would leave such instructions with the assurance that they would be carried out even if I had to work all night or even pray all night for the success of the service.

When such instructions come, the man of God expects you to carry them out as efficiently as possible. A typical example is if he asks for a report on the statistics, events etc. of one of the ministries of the church. Apart from typing out the report, you could also prepare a presentation package. As you submit your typed paper report, you also attach your software presentation package to it. I tell you, your response to his request will inform the man of God about you and your role as an Armor Bearer. It gives him the confidence that the work is being carried out with efficiency, initiative and excellence.

God depends on you and I to properly execute all that He has committed into our hands.

x) A Pillar: Pillars support the structure, keeping it from collapse, deterioration and/or damage. People sometimes bring so much disorder in the house of God that damage invariably is a result. As a pillar in the house of God, ensure that this damage is not done.

The average man or woman goes through challenges and rough times during the week either at work, school or in the community, and the only place they feel they can express themselves or let go is in the church. For example, some Christians desire to indulge in gossip but their office rules prevent them from indulging in such at work.

As Sister A consistently gossips with Sister B in the Church every Sunday, they disturb the services especially during Sunday schools, and thereby grieve the Holy Spirit. They sometimes do not participate because of their side talking and gossips, and hinder others from concentrating on the Word of God. Such must be stopped, and pillar of service must enforce order in the church.

The Word of God is sharp, requiring alertness and an inattentive person could easily miss his/her blessing of that day. A wrong action could cause a person to miss the voice of God, not because God did not speak to them, but because he was too busy doing irrelevant things during services and so did not hear God. Watch out for such people in our churches and ask the Holy Spirit to help you deal with them accordingly and in love.

As a Pillar you are required to prevent the house of God from becoming a subject of damage or destruction. Some children of God feel being in their father's house permits them to act without repercussions. Uzziah wanted to help God by supporting the ark of covenant without permission and he landed in the graveyard just for that action.

A sister was invited to our local church during the christening of a child and in her effort to carry out the video coverage of the event; she became disorderly, causing a lot of distraction in the church. Upon noticing this I promptly called her to order, informing her that she required permission to cover the event and would have to limit her movement during the service. Of course she took offence on the grounds that this was the House of God, and she could do whatever she liked. No Sir or Ma'am is the appropriate response for such people and you must enforce order by reminding them that there are rules and regulations in the house of God.

Also the filth we see in the house of God sometimes makes you wonder if people are actually ready for the heavenly places our Lord Jesus Christ promised. In heaven there is no dirt or littering of the floors or chairs. Our churches now have become storage facilities for jackets, toys, feeding bottles, children's clothes, Bibles etc., and no wonder Jesus was so angry when they turned the house of prayer to den of thieves. He promptly brought order into the temple.

The assorted items that are left behind in church after services are amazing, and you may even find bubble gum sticking to the seats in churches. We sometimes spend a lot of money to get the carpet clean just because of a few unruly people in the house of God. As a Pillar do not allow these things in the church, always bring correction when it is noticed. The Lord will help His church Amen.

The use of cell phones in our churches during the services is an increasing problem. Anyone in the house of God with an instrument of distraction has become a vessel in hands of Devil. One ring of the cell phone should prompt the owner to turn it off but people often don't! I have been present in church when a cell phone must have rung up to four times before the owner seemingly unperturbed, picked up the call and began to speak even as she walked out of the sanctuary. My goodness, this is unacceptable in our Father's house, and you must always call such people to order.

If you are guilty of this, you must realize that whoever is calling during church service for a chat is not a godly friend. If the case is that urgent, a message can be left. Most of the time what seems urgent is not really an emergency, but just intended to instill "fear" in you. Fear stands for the acronym FEAR - False Evidence Appearing Real.

✠ ✠ ✠

Chapter Six

PROTOCOL OFFICERS

Concerning the affairs of God there is a lot of protocol to follow. When proper protocol is not observed we miss the mindset of God concerning that situation. When Moses encountered the presence of God in Exodus 3: 4-5 three things were obvious:

> *"And when the Lord saw that he turned aside to see, God called him out of the midst of the bush, and said Moses, Moses. And he said. Here am I. And he said, Draw not nigh hither: put off thy shoes from off thy feet, for the place whereon thou standest is holy ground"*

First, God called Moses, secondly, God told Moses to stop where he was and thirdly, God told Moses to take off his shoes. If Moses had failed any of these protocol steps, it could have been the end of Prophet Moses. Imagine what God's fire would have done to him.

Many people in the church of God today do not observe protocol, invariably missing their blessings, and getting discouraged in the pursuit of destiny. Many people have actually sustained injuries because they did not observe protocol in the things of God, e.g. Uzziah who met an untimely death. Certain things matter to God, they invariably bring honor and maintain order to His church.

Who are those to enforce God's protocol? Protocol Officers in the church are **called** into this **office**. There is a difference between office and a call and if you hold an office in the house of God without a calling you will bring disorderliness into the house of God.

Nehemiah was a good example of a Protocol Officer called to rebuild and at the same time maintain order in the house of God. God singled him out to lead and build, and he was focused. There were more than enough people in prominent offices that God could have called for this assignment but they were too full of themselves. Such people lacked focus and direction and later became agents of the devil to distract the set man assigned to build and maintain order.

This is an office that brings a lot of leadership visibility, and you cannot afford to pay attention to the things of the flesh, to the detriment of the spirit. The Bible tells us in John 4 that God is a Spirit and those who will worship Him must do so in Spirit and in truth. If you are not subject to the things of the Spirit, you will be unable to maintain order in the house of God.

For those who are called into this office, you must take your eyes off the title, pay more attention to service and concentrate on the Lord. The Holy Spirit brings out the best in you when you put your trust in Him and are willing to receive clear instructions on what to do concerning any programs or regular Sunday services.

God's mercies are new everyday, and he inspires new things in our churches. Stereotyped activities and the same predictable service pattern every Sunday such that the people can almost predict what the Pastors, Ministers, and Choir will do is not acceptable before God. Moses got clear instructions for the children of Israel but as they journeyed out of Egypt, God gave fresh instructions on how to proceed. In observing protocol before God you must expect to receive directions.

In our respective churches, there are people (Protocol Officers) who have been assigned to be the first point of contact with other ministries or ministers. They are in charge of caring for the Guest Ministers from the point of arriving for special programs up until the point of departure.

SPECIAL PROGRAMS

It will be necessary to spend some time to examine the planning, organizing and implementing of special programs. A lot of errors are made here. When a special program is decided upon, and the Guest Minister is announced, what should follow after is spiritual preparation.

i) Prayer and Fasting
Fasting should be carried out at all levels of the church and information on this should be adequately communicated to all departments and the church body for proper preparation. More

importantly this becomes a prayer burden within the intercessory team or the prayer ministry.

Prayerful preparations will prevent poor performance. When you have poor performance, some may say, **"Perhaps that was how God wanted it."** Absolutely not, because our God is a God of perfection as the psalmist declares Psalm 138:8 – *"Thou O Lord will perfect everything that concerns me."* It is very important to prayerfully prepare the church for the program with a spirit of excellence.

Having fully committed the programs into God's hands through prayer and fasting, it is important to get the information across to all house fellowships in order to reach church members who were not in church when it was announced and those who are not church members but are in fellowship with the church.

ii) Provision of Quality Handbills

Many people decide whether or not to attend a church program merely by looking at the flyer or handbill and yet some churches take for granted this medium of advertisement. Pastors need to invest in the printing of materials for their day-to-day church needs and special programs. The handbills for example, speak for themselves. It is a lie of the Devil that you have to be a big church to have enough money for sophisticated publications. God is beautiful and when we set our hearts to do something decent for the Lord, He will make the provision.

Several Pastors have testified that some members of their churches, after seeing beautiful handbills printed by their own local church decided to pay for subsequent ones. One Pastor reported that they experienced an increase in membership after a successful conference in the church. He said the preparations, starting from intense prayer to beautiful handbills etc. paid off. Research shows however that only few church members invite people for programs in their local churches for several reasons. Don't let poor handbills be one of the excuses.

iii) One-on-one telephone invitation and reminders

This is one of the most effective ways in getting people to church or special programs. While it is good enough to give out handbills, it is also better to follow up with phone calls. This conveys a sense of interest and caring in the life of the invitee. My Pastor encourages and welcomes this procedure whenever we have special programs and it works all the time. Visitors are called special guests, and you can have special guests not just during special programs but also during regular church services. When you invite special guests and you tell them to specifically request your attention upon arrival to the program or service, it will be very difficult for such a person to say no. These are tested procedures that have helped ministries to grow over the years.

iv) Personal Follow-up visitation

Extending your invitation and one-on-one telephone follow-up reminders are all unique ways of making sure that your guest shows up for the program but personal follow-up visitation is a more guaranteed way to ensure attendance. Taking time to visit a person few days to the program sends a message of importance and relevance of such program in the life of the person. Expressions like *"Don't miss this great opportunity"* etc. will remain with your invitee until day of the program and Holy Spirit will perfect the rest. God expects His children to reach out to those still searching for the truth. Remember that the Devil will fight to make sure you don't succeed because his ministry is to deprive God's children of their blessings during these programs.

v) Saturday night or Sunday morning church rallies.

These are final preparations prior to the day of the program, to enhance the success of the program. Here you must rally church members to participate in the exercise. It can be combined with announcement using battery powered public address system and distribution of hand bills.

vi) Final Review: You go over what every member of the planning/protocol team has been able to accomplish prior to that day and amendments and/or lapses would be addressed at this stage and not on the day, or a few hours before the program. Delay costs a lot of time, wasted efforts and resources. Every body brings to the review table all that they have done and final prayers are said for God to move. Elijah asked one of the wives of the sons of prophet what she had at home and she said nothing but a jar of oil. That was her preparation for greatness.

✠ ✠ ✠

Chapter Seven

SERVANT LEADERSHIP

It is important at this stage to introduce the principle of leadership ordained by our Lord and Master, Jesus Christ that should make your service reasonable and acceptable to Him. It is this that will not cause your work to be burnt by fire, because every work shall pass through God's fire of testing. We see this principle revealed and established to us in the Gospel According to Mark Chapter 10 verse 43 to 44 and it reads:

> *"But so shall it not be among you: but whosoever will be great among you, shall be your minister: And whosoever of you will be the chiefest, shall be servant of all."*

The word minister in that verse means servant – one who is called to serve or provide service. Whichever way you look at it, he is not called to be served but to serve. This is the Masters' master principle and it is known as *Servant Leadership or Servant hood*. This principle completely contradicts the world's idea of leadership. Leadership in the world's system places a man on a pedestal wherein he is highly exalted, served, and all privileges are reposed in him. But in God's domain where His children are called to serve it is *"…so shall it not be among you:.."*

Many of God's children who had had this understanding served with this at the back of their minds and were not ashamed to declare it. The chief amongst them was Paul the Apostle who called himself "a bond slave" or "bond servant of the Lord" and he indeed served going through all sorts of afflictions that servant hood brought through his path. These he calls light affliction. Even Prophet Moses he whom God used to lead millions of Jews out of Egypt started as a servant and ended as a servant. While the world interprets servant hood as low and degrading, in the kingdom of God the servant of God is viewed as a great person.

it might not proceed out of their mouth but their countenance shows it all the time.

Some are called to lead Sunday school classes of 20 students and the proceeds of their leadership are a bunch of frustrated students. Rather for them to be servant they are been served. What about the newly ordained deacons and deaconess, the assistant pastors and elders. Some are considered as fast track leaders, they want the title so much yet they do not cultivate the spirit of servant hood.

In the Gospel According to Mark chapter 10 verse 37 to 40, two disciples came to Jesus and "*They said unto him, Grant unto us that we may sit, one on thy right hand, and the other on thy left hand in thy glory.*" These men James and John the sons of Zebedee in collaboration with their mum wanted leadership on a platter of gold. They desired the accolade, grandeur and plaudit that it attracts with neither the responsibility nor the price tag. The Lord aptly told them of a cup they needed to drink from in order for their requests to be granted. This necessary cup of pruning in service contains endurance, hardship, dependency, abstinence, longsuffering, patience, denials, love and some heavy doses of "light afflictions" (apologies to Apostle Paul). Of course, they later in life drank of the cup by paying the price with their lives.

Many in position of maintaining order and leadership in the church today are unaware of this cup, and even when they are, they are unprepared and unwilling to drink from it. I heard story about a brother who was called into the office of a deacon and exactly one week later a fellow parishioner referred to this leader as 'brother' during a church meeting, the honorable deacon flared up and replied immediately, cautioning, and interrupting the brother and explaining to him the reason why he must be properly addressed as a deacon and not as a brother. I wonder how far he will go leading the people of God.

Apostle Paul through out his ministry led by serving the church, community, and cities, no wonder he left a legacy we talk about till this day. We see the same set of standards revealed as we read the bible. For example, in the book of Acts of the Apostles Chapter 6 verses 3-4 when some deacons were to be appointed these words were declared to make the choice

".. wherefore, brethren, look ye out among you seven men of honest report, full of Holy

Ghost and wisdom, whom we may appoint over this business. But we will give ourselves continually to prayer, and to the ministry of the word."

From scriptures, you could identify the manner and condition necessary to appoint a leader to an office. They must be men of honest report, wisdom and full of the Holy Spirit. Not by chance or how long they have been in church or the ministry. These are the yard sticks for many and the consequences are severe - no order in church. These vital requirements usher us to the importance of the role of the Holy Spirit in service. This we shall thoroughly examine in the next chapter.

✣ ✣ ✣

Chapter Eight

THE ROLE OF THE HOLY SPIRIT
IN THE SERVICE

It would be inappropriate to conclude this book without discussing the importance of the Holy Spirit in all these previously outlined ministries. John 14: 26 says,

> *"But the Comforter, which is the Holy Ghost, whom the Father will send in my name, he shall teach you all things, and bring all things to your remembrance, whatsoever I have said unto you."*

The Bible tells us that the Holy Spirit is our guide, helper, and teacher. He was sent by the Lord to make our lives and ministries run according to God's divine plan and purpose. A person who functions in any of these ministries that is not subject to the Holy Spirit will have a tendency to struggle in his call and ministry.

The Holy Spirit empowers a believer to do exploits in his specific assignment to God. "*They that know their God shall be strong and do exploits*" A believer with experience and the influence of the Holy Spirit will function beyond the ordinary. People around such a person will testify of his exemplary and outstanding service to God. That person will enjoy and benefit from divine information and guidance that will cause him to be outstanding. One is at a great risk without the presence of the Holy Spirit because one's individual strength is insufficient for survival in your ministry – "*..Not by might, nor by power, but by my spirit, saith the Lord*" - Zechariah 4: 6.

The Holy Spirit equips and prepares an Usher, Armor Bearer or Protocol Officer for service. A man called Bezaleel in Exodus 31: 3 manifested great understanding, wisdom and knowledge in all manner of workmanship because the Holy Spirit adequately supplied him with resources. When a man who prepares for an examination and days before, the Holy Spirit begins to zero in on specific areas of studies, such a person will enter the exam room with boldness and confidence.

The Holy Spirit is our guide and so we need Him at all times to direct our path so that we don't lose focus in our pursuit of destiny. The gospel of John 16: 3 says *"the Holy Spirit will guide you into all truth…"* as Apostle Paul was guided in his missionary journeys in Acts 16: 6-7.

The book of Psalm chapter 46 verse 1 says the Holy Spirit is *"…a very present help in trouble"* One of the largest gatherings of believers in the world is the Congress of the Redeemed Christian Church of God held annually at the Redemption Camp in Nigeria West Africa with an average attendance numbering about eight to eleven million people. There is no doubt that the Holy Spirit is the helper at this program because in all these years, there have never been reports of stampedes, disorderliness etc. This could not have been by the power or skill of the Ushers, Protocol Officers, Armor Bearers etc., but of the Holy Spirit definitely at work.

The leading of the Holy Spirit is paramount, and Romans 8: 14 says, *"For as many as are led by the*

Spirit of God, they are the sons of God". Consequently, Ushers, Protocol Officers, Armor Bearers etc. who are not led by the Spirit of God cannot be sons and daughters of God and will have no legal standing to maintain order in His Church.

For as many that are called in the ministries of Ushering, Protocol Officers, Armor Bearing etc., God is depending on you to be subject to the Holy Spirit for empowerment to **"Maintain Order in the Church"**.

God bless you.

REFERENCES

1) Ushering 101 & Greeters 101 by Reverend Buddy Bell

2) Lean on Me by Steve Akoni

3) Serving as a Church Greeter by Leslie Parrott. Paul E. Engle, series editor

4) Serving by Safeguarding your Church by Robert H. Welch. Paul E. Engle series editor.

It is very important to note that all the ministries outlined in the early chapters are categorized as leadership roles. The word leader or leadership to certain people who find themselves in the ministry of ushering, armor bearing and protocol could mean different things to them and I am inspired to write and explain who a true leader is especially if they are going to maintain order in the church.

It is quite humbling to be a servant in Gods house as God's service demands unalloyed humility, commitment and responsibility. The Lord Jesus had to make himself clear by physically demonstrating it and also verbalizing the same in the presence of all his disciples. This could be demoralizing for these men who had perceived him to be the Messiah king and they, his right hand men who would together with him enjoy the gains of leadership. So in John Chapter 13 verse 5 we read:

> *"After that he poureth water into the basin, and began to wash the disciples' feet, and wipe them with the towel wherewith he was girded. Then cometh Simon Peter: and Peter saith unto him, Lord, dost thou wash my feet?"*

This account above was a remarkable experience he shared with His disciples. One day the leader they long referred to as master began to wash their feet. This to some of them or should I say all was an abomination. How can this be? Is Jesus alright? These were some of the expressions of the disciples. But Jesus seeing the future of these men as leaders and enforcers of order in churches and cities needed to educate them on their positions. And he taught them with a "visible demonstration or action" that was going to make them distinguished leaders who would truly serve.

WHO IS A LEADER?

A leader is someone who leads and serves others.

A leader is someone who knows the road, keeps ahead of the road and leads others

A leader helps others find their lift

A leader as a change agent-maintains and enforces order

We have many leaders now in the church who have zeal to serve but lack knowledge. All they seek is popularity and fame. Such a leader could even acquire knowledge but wrongly apply them in their roles. This becomes disastrous in their handling of brethren and maintaining order in the church.

The book of 2 Sam Chapter 18 verses 19 to 32 illustrates two leaders who had zeal to serve but one lacked information and understanding and the result was very embarrassing. While Cushi had the vital message to pass across, this was not true of Ahimaaz the son of Zadok who even though outran Cushi to the presence of the king got there with nothing concrete. And the king told him to turn aside and stand still until the right person with the correct message would come. Even though Cushi came in much later, he had the message and as he divulged the content of his message it made the necessary impact on his hearers. We can see here that Ahimaaz demonstrated zeal but without knowledge *"For I bear them record that they have zeal of God, but not according to knowledge."* Rom 10: 2

A true leader is servant, one who uses his God given gift to serve others and not Lord it over them. One who is teachable, rebukable, correctable and humble. What we see now in our churches are unbroken leaders who are given responsibilities of leadership and enforcers of order.

The outcome of their leadership in the long run is always chaotic, unruly, unattractive, and unacceptable. Their way and manner of conducting business in the house of God has turned many away from the church. Their reprehensible and arrogant behaviors have killed the inspiration of many who want to be part of the Lord's house. May God help us from such men.

A leader leads by serving. Prophet Elisha, one of the most successful leaders in bible days led the sons of the prophets by serving them. Moses the deliverer of God's people also did the same. Read below what God called him in the book of Joshua chapter one verse one

> *"Now after the death of Moses the servant of the Lord it came to pass, that the Lord spake unto Joshua the son of Nun Moses' minister...".*

Notice he was called *"Moses the servant of the Lord..."* This same Moses lead hundreds of thousand of people for several years through thick and thin situation in the wilderness and with all his great doing the Lord referred to him as a servant. You dare not call some servant in the church of today, it will be considered as an insult. Though